Michael Sandford

Rock Springs

Arizona

HISTORY SERIES

MICHAEL SANDFORD
FORWARD TERRY EARP

Black & white photos courtesy of the Warner family
Color photos are property of the author
Third & Fourth edition layout & editor LeeAnn Sharpe
Produced by Strawberry Productions
Published by Crazy Cowgirl Publications

First Edition
ISBN-13: 978-1482549997
ISBN-10: 1482549999
Library of Congress: pending Copyright: SR1-865600595

Second Edition
ISBN-13: 978-1484144848
ISBN-10: 1484144848

Third Edition
ISBN-13: 978-1490389417
ISBN-10: 1490389415

Fourth Edition - B/W Edition
ISBN-13: 978-1492701422
ISBN-10: 1492701424

TESTIMONIALS

Dolan Ellis says: Bob, I just wanted to thank you for sending me the copy of Michael Sandford's book, "Rock Springs, Arizona". I emailed both of you guys to say thanks. I have a special interest in Rock Springs. To me, it is one of the precious and unrecognized historical spots in the state. Most of our population today think of Rock Springs as a place of great pies, down home cookin' and "get down fun". I think of it that way, too. But for me, it runs much deeper. When I think about the generations upon generations of people who have stopped there to find comfort and rest, it sends my mind a-flyin'. I see the shadows and the tracks of those people out of Arizona history...from our ancient prehistoric Indians, to mountain men, pioneer families, women with babies, cowboys, stage coaches, outlaws, military soldiers, prospectors, secret lovers, and not so secret lovers. Imagine...if those rocks could only speak, the stories they could tell! I will enjoy having the book in my collection of Arizona things. Thanks again.
Dolan Ellis

See Dolan's latest CD at **www.dolanellis.net**

Bob Roloff says: Mike Sandford has done a great job through Warner family research putting this book together. This is the only book ever published on the history of Rock Springs, and a follow up 2nd book is in the works. Mike has a previous book "The Last Stagecoach Ride", (See Page 139) describing a harrowing stagecoach ride from Prescott to Phoenix down the "old Black Canyon Highway". A short fun read.

Marshall Trimble says: The first time I saw Rock Springs was in October, 1947. I was eight years old. The Depression had left us without that proverbial pot. Dad had recently sold the cows and hired out as a fireman on the Peavine, the nickname for that winding Santa Fe Railroad line that ran from Ash Fork to Phoenix. We packed up our meager belongings, hooked up an old two-room trailer house to the 1936 Ford V8 and headed north.

The only paved road from Phoenix to Ash Fork in those days was U.S. 89 by way of Wickenburg and Prescott. There was one major obstacle, Yarnell Hill, and that old Ford couldn't make the grade pulling a trailer house.

So, our only choice was to head north on Mission Drive (27th Avenue) then travel the old stagecoach road now being called Black Canyon Highway that headed north towards the New River Station where the pavement ended and a gravel road began.

We stopped at Rock Springs for water and gas then crossed the Agua Fria and up the narrow, winding road north of the river that is still visible today from I-17.

About halfway up the grade the clutch blew out and we had to be towed into Bumble Bee by a highway department dump truck. All there was to Bumble Bee in those days were some small cabins, a school and the general store that included a gas station, café, bar, groceries and hardware. It was also the area's social gathering place and on Saturday nights they pushed back the tables and had a dance.

My dad flagged down a southbound car and gave some money and a parts list to the driver to drop off at Mr. Hilding's garage on 27th Avenue. Mr. Hilding, filled the order and gave it to another driver heading north.

When the parts arrived dad went about re-building the clutch while my brothers and I passed the time pretending to be gold prospectors and exploring the country around Bumble Bee. We carefully avoided the school for fear of being abducted and enrolled during our unscheduled vacation.

After making repairs we loaded up and headed north from Bumble Bee only to break down again on that steep hill leading out of Crazy Basin just south of Cordes.

Henry Cordes had a gas station and general store similar to the one at Bumble Bee and he became our host for a few more days while more parts arrived from Phoenix.

The journey to Mayer, Dewey and Prescott was uneventful as there were no more steep hills to climb. We turned on U.S. 89 north of Prescott and made our way the final 53 miles to Ash Fork. It would be my home for the next eight years.

Each time I drive up the mountain to Sunset Point my eyes always drift over to that narrow road that winds its way up from Rock Springs to Bumble Bee. I was too young to appreciate the history as we traveled along that old stagecoach road but it did leave me with vivid memories. Proof of that lies in the fact that more than 60 years later I still remember that eight-day journey as if it was only yesterday.

Marshall Trimble
Arizona State Historian

Augie Perry current Rock Springs owner and general manager says: There is a certain stewardship that's involved in running it, (Rock Springs Café) both as a business, which is vital and critical, and at the same time trying to contribute to Arizona history.

ABOUT THE COVER

"This is today's main dining room at Rock Springs Café," says Bonnie Warner, *"before Bob and Mary (Warner) made this a restaurant after Dad had passed."*

"When I was 12 to 16 my Dad had made this into a bar. People would buy their beer, or whatever, at the store and take it here where we had a bar and tables."

"The family would make sandwiches, if the customer needed. On weekends during the day we had a band, an accordion player and a guitar player. They would come up from Phoenix and play. So did some of the customers. Dad would put up signs around town and along the way to Phoenix. Everyone always had fun. We also had a juke box."

Cover Photo
Cowboys from Wranglers Roost, New River in 1940, ride in to Rock Springs. The rider far left is Pete Halle, who supplied the photo. The Halle family owned Wranglers Roost from 1941 into the 50's.

Back Cover Upper - Rock Springs circa 1946

Back Cover Lower - Rock Springs circa 2012

ABOUT THE AUTHOR

Michael Sandford is a 50+ years Arizonian who has made the Black Canyon area his home. He held various positions from Phoenix to Black Canyon via several mining towns that are no longer on the map.

Michael's desire to present documented factual history started as a teen, writing articles for newspapers such as the Black Canyon Times, and Arizona Republic. Later Canyon Country News, published by Robert Helgeson and Foothills Focus, published by John Alexander, as a free-lance photographer and reporter for over 3 years.

He has researched and written about Arizona history, for better than twenty-five years, with his work published in many Arizona newspapers.

His representation of Rock Springs is documented and factual from the view of the Warner family.

He is one of three founding members of the Black Canyon Historical Society. Elizabeth Wright and Robert Helgeson founded the society with Sandford, however, Sandford is the only one living.

He is the author of *"Black Canyon City - A Thimble of History"* published 1998. He also is an award winning poet and photographer. His most recent book of poetry titled, *"Knick Knacks and Notions"* was published 1999. His latest history story, *"The Last Stagecoach Ride"* is based upon a true story. (See Page 139)

IN MEMORY OF
TERRY SANDFORD

FORWARD

TERRY EARP

Many of us pass a tiny town like Rock Springs and seldom give it a second thought or second glance. Too often these places are no more than a spot along the road to grab a quick bite or gas on the way to our destination.

Yes, few of us stop to think that these places also have a history filled with stories and personalities. After reading Mike Sandford's book on how and why Rock Springs came to be, I came away with an appreciation of Rock Springs as its own little town. I hope you will too.

TERRY EARP

TABLE OF CONTENTS

LIST OF ILLUSTRATIONS

PRELUDE

Arizona Territorial Military Locations mid to late 1800's.

Throughout the territorial period, the area now known as Rock Springs was in the center of major routes between the northern & southern regions of Arizona Territory and the central route between the Mohave region of California and the Pueblo lands in New Mexico.

Today it is the center point between Phoenix and Prescott and a major rest stop for travelers on Interstate 17.

Rock Springs is also the halfway point between Phoenix and Flagstaff. Summer and winter travel between the three cities make Rock Springs a central point for travelers needing a break whether it is for food, gas, pies, or just to rest and relax.

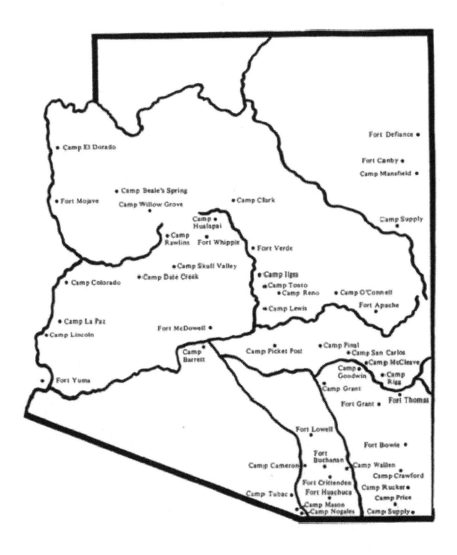

Military Posts of Arizona Territory

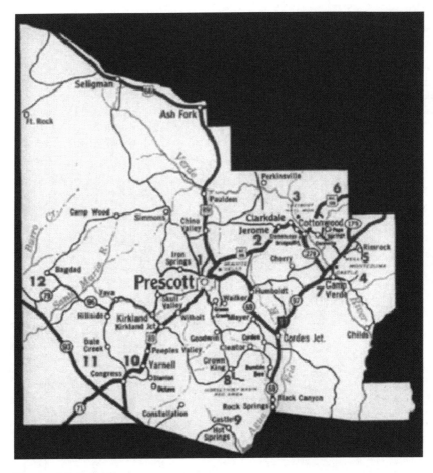

Yavapai County

Rock Springs is located at the southern edge of Yavapai County in Central Arizona. It is on the SR-69 portion of I-17.

These pictures represent a portion of Rock Springs history.

View from island on I-17

Photo by Bob Roloff "The Arizona Duuude"

Mike and Linda discussing Rock Springs history

Photo by Bob Roloff "The Arizona Duuude"

The Rock Spring – natural outcrop of water

Photo by Bob Roloff "The Arizona Duuude"

Rock Springs Patio

Much of Rock Springs history is tied to the nearby Kay Copper Mine.

Kay Copper Mine, consisted of 153 claims stretching over 3,182 acres including, mill acreage of 590 acres.

Stock certificates were known to be issued at least through 1928, as displayed in the attached certificate. The value of the certificates return decreased when the Kay Copper Company was thrown into bankruptcy.

The company ceased to exist in 1931.

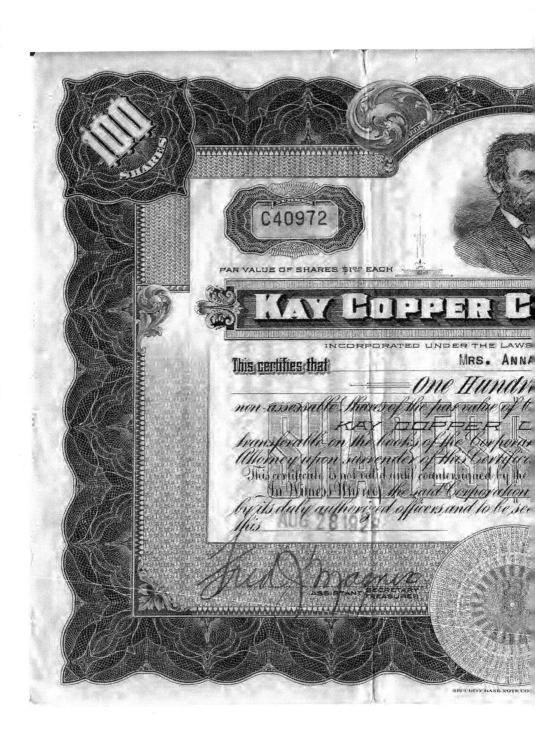

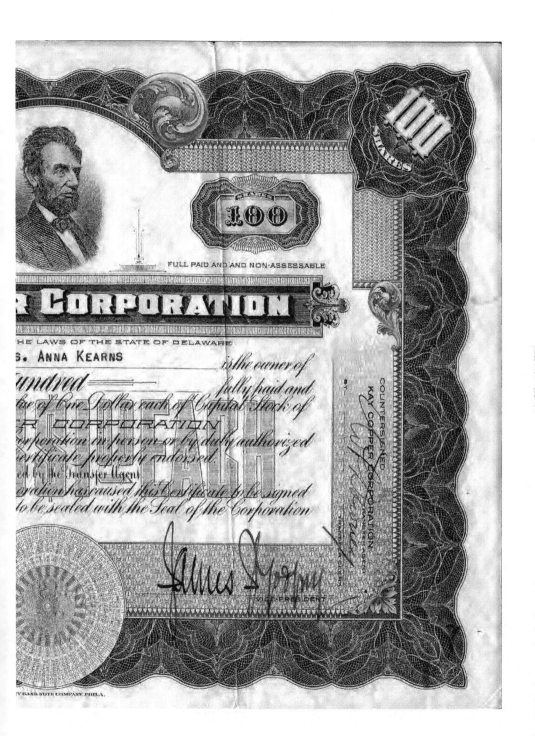

100 SHARES

STARE 100

FULL PAID AND AND NON-ASSESSABLE

R CORPORATION

HE LAWS OF THE STATE OF DELAWARE

S. ANNA KEARNS is the owner of

undred fully paid and

the of One Dollar each of Capital Stock of

R CORPORATION

oration in person or by duly authorized

ertificate properly endorsed.

ed by the Transfer Agent

oration has caused this Certificate to be signed

to be sealed with the Seal of the Corporation

COUNTERSIGNED
KAY COPPER CORPORATION

VICE-PRESIDENT

BANK NOTE COMPANY, PHILA.

31

ROCK SPRINGS ARIZONA YAVAPAI COUNTY

Through the years, many authors have written about Rock Springs, Arizona, where the springs flow through the rocks. The settlers and military patrols of the 1860's watered their horses and other beasts of burden at these springs.

Native pottery unearthed in Black Canyon area.

Records of this location go further back in time to when Southern Illinois University, Professor George Gumerman, and his team of archaeological students, explored Native American artifacts here and through the State in the early 1980's. These records date back 1,400 years, as the Rock Springs area was once littered with chards, metates, and other artifacts. There are no artifacts left; all were be removed, by time bandits, through recent years.

This compiled history of Rock Springs is of recent times and about how the Warner family settled Rock Springs, in the early 1920's. In addition to State and Yavapai County records, it includes information passed on by the family of Benjamin Warner about the early settlers and business owners in Cañon.

Author's Note

It is this author's belief that if it were not for Benjamin Warner, the community of today's Black Canyon City, may not have existed.

- *Ben Warner was not the first to build a general store in Black Canyon, a.k.a. Cañon. There was Charles Goddard, followed by William Martin.*
- *He was not the first land developer. It was Martin.*
- *He was not the first farmer. There was Martin, the Mannifees' and others.*
- *He did not create the electoral district. It was Charles Goddard.*
- *He was not the first school Superintendent. It was Charles Goddard. (1894)*
- *He built his business "Rock Springs" Hotel with a view, a pool & dance hall, gas station, general store for the locals, and short order restaurant.*
- *Warner sold land and cattle too. He was actively involved in the schools development of modern times. Warner was school superintendent in the 1940's.*
- *Without Ben Warner, most likely, the nearby community of Black Canyon City may not have existed.*

BENJAMIN WARNER
THE EARLY YEARS

Benjamin Warner was born January 12, 1892, in Cleveland, Ohio, son of John and Christine Warner. Benjamin was the youngest of four children; two boys and two girls. Benjamin's parents were the children of immigrants, who came from the old world, settling in Pennsylvania. John's birth name was, Anton Kalish. He and his parents came from Poland. Christine's birth name was, Julia Tarkowlkwi. She came with her parents from Germany. Like many immigrants, the parents changed their name to conform to the American Society.

They moved from Pennsylvania and settled in Cleveland, Ohio, where John was a blacksmith. They eventually moved to the village of Benton Ridge, in Hancock County, a small farming community, where they raised their family. John saw to it the children were well educated.

Benjamin[1] grew up working on the railroad and eventually, became a conductor. He invested his earnings into rental properties. As the United States entered WWI in 1917, Benjamin joined the Navy. When the war ended, Ben returned home and continued to work on the railroad.

---

[1] Family Record- Oral family history

Somewhere around the time of 1918, Ben was in a horrible car accident, where someone died, according to his son Robert.[2]

Ben Warner 1915

---

[2] It is unknown if this was a friend or family in his car or a victim in another car.

In 1919, Ben came to Arizona, working for Arizona Power Company, laying power lines through Arizona. Although the family members preferred Ben stay in Ohio, Ben felt the need to make a new start in life, so move to Arizona he did.

He was living in Mayer, Arizona, in 1920, working for the Arizona Power Company as a lineman. Ben looked at the needs of the people who lived in the surrounding area of the small mining communities, such as Gillett, Mayer, Bumble Bee, and Cañon[3]. The Black Canyon area was rich in gold, silver and copper. As the twentieth century grew, so did the opportunities in this area.

[3] Cañon became Black Canyon

ELECTRICITY COMES TO BLACK CANYON

By 1900, most major cities in the U.S. and Territories were developing electricity into civilization. In 1881, Tombstone had a telephone. In 1898, the Congress Mine, at Congress Junction, was the first mine in Arizona Territory, to use electricity in its operations.

In 1919, Ben Warner got a job with the Arizona Power Company, laying power lines across Arizona. The linemen rode horses or mules from Mayer where they stayed in one of the rental apartments.

Young Ben Warner at Squaw Valley Ranch, owned by future in-laws, the Jones.

They began working in the Black Canyon area. Ben saw the area as a future place for growth and other opportunities.

This is where he met Ruby Jones.

James Jones and family[4] came from the Tonto Basin area by way of Texas. They homesteaded in Cañon, in an area known as Squaw Valley, where they built a ranch in 1916.

The power company set up camp at the springs. This is also where the power station was built. People other than the employees would often come to buy supplies from the company store.

Martin's General Store

There was Martin's General Store, north of the area of Rock Springs, in Cañon. His general store was an old wooden stagecoach station and Post Office. His merchandise was priced high.

Ben noticed this and knew he could give customers better prices than Martin's store or sending them to Gillett, or Bumble Bee.

---

[4] Family Record- Oral family history

As the power company was preparing to move to the south, toward Phoenix, Ben developed an idea. He talked things over with his foreman John Poss, about the aspects of operating a general store out of the company tent. Ben also observed that with the establishment of the new power stations, they had to be near a major thoroughfare where they were recorded on maps. This aided him in advertisement and access to customers in this location, near the newly completed power station.

The Arizona Power Company left the area, moved south west leaving Ben and another co-worker to work the power lines. At the springs location, there was also a lineman's shack[5] that stored Ben's merchandise and company materials for the electrical operations. In October of 1921, Arizona Power Company left the area and Ben laid claim to the land commonly known as Rock Springs.

As the year wore on Ben proposed to Ruby and they were married, January 3. 1922, in Phoenix. Ben and Ruby lived in the company tent, developing their general store, as Ben continued working for the power company.

The rest of 1922, was a busy year for the Warner's. Ben discovered gold on their newly claimed land, and on February 20, 1922, he filed his gold claim for the Rock Springs land.

---

[5] Family History

Notice of Mining Location
LODE CLAIM

To All Whom It May Concern:

This Mining Claim, the name of which is the _Rock Springs_ Mining Claim, situated on lands belonging to the United States of America, and in which there are valuable mineral deposits, was entered upon and located for the purpose of exploration and purchase by _B Warner_ _Citizens_

the undersigned, on the _20_ day of _Feb_ 19 _22_

The length of this claim is _1300_ feet and _0_ claim _200_ feet in a _East_ direction and _1300_ feet in a _West_ direction from the center of the discovery shaft, of which the notice is posted, lengthwise of the claim, together with _300_ feet in width of the surface grounds, on each side of the center of said claim. The general course of the lode deposit and position is from the _East_ to the _West_

The claim is staked and marked in the _Square C. G. L._ Mining District, in Yavapai County, in the State of Arizona, about _1 mile_ in a _Easterly_ direction from .... and 2 miles in a southeasterly direction .... on the Phoenix road

The .... upon the ground as follows: Beginning at .... monument of stone

at a point to .... direction _200_ feet from the discovery shaft .... center of the _east_ end line of said claim; thence .... feet to a _monument of stone_ .... _northwest_ corner of said claim; thence .... feet to a _monument_ being at the .... of said claim; thence _200_ feet at the center of the _west_ end of said claim; .... feet in a _a monument_ being at the .... corner of said claim; thence _1300_ .... feet to a _monument_ at the _southwest_ corner of said claim; thence .... feet to the place of beginning.

All done under the provisions of Chapter Six, of Title XXXII, of the Revised Statutes of the United States, and of an Act of the General Assembly of Arizona, entitled "An Act to Revise and Codify the Laws of the Territory of Arizona," approved March 16, 1901.

Dated and posted on the grounds this _20_ day of _Feb_ 19 _22_

....
Witness

B Warner

Filed and recorded at request of _Ben Warner_ April 12-th A.D. 19 22 at _9.00_ o'clock _a_ M., Book 120 of Mines, page _448_, Records of Yavapai County, Arizona.

(SEAL) _E A McSwiggin_, County Recorder.

By ...., Deputy Recorder.

Claim for Lode Filing by Ben Warner 1922

Their first child Robert Norman was born, October 17th, 1922. Since he was still working with Arizona Power Company and living in a tent at Rock Springs, the newborn accelerated Ben's goal to complete the vision he had of Rock Springs.

As part of expanding the purpose of the land use and building their homestead, they got a small herd of cattle, most likely believed from his in-laws, to help build their ranch. This region was 'open range' and a brand was necessary. Ben filed for his brand so he would not lose his cattle on the open range.

Their brand was filed through the Coconino Sun, December 1, 1922, as the lazy A D.

The Coconino sun. (Flagstaff, Ariz.) 1898-1978, December 01, 1922, Page Page Ten, Image 10

⟨D   C right hip   Ben Warner
       H right shoulder   Canon Arizona

Ben Warner's Lazy A D Brand

As the homestead grew into 1923, Ben asked business associate John Gabriel to help him build Rock Springs buildings. Gabriel's nickname, "Mutt" was how most people in Cañon knew him.

Mutt lived east of the Agua Fria, near the thumb where he had a sheep ranch. He was also an excellent concrete craftsman and stone mason. Ben and John, made masonry concrete blocks, on site and began building the General Store, adding on top a hotel.

Gabriel would years later, assist in building the extension to New River Station, and help with the building of the Sun-Up Ranch.

Enter 1924, with the birth of Ben Jr., on January 3. As the year progresses, Ben leaves his work behind at the Arizona Power Company, to run his own business as Rock Springs General Store. Ben begins to build the house for his family.

Ben's father, brother and sisters[6], felt it would be impossible for building a business and family when Ben went west. They felt Ben would squander his money and go broke. At the family's insistence, Ben left his investments in his older sister's hands.

This initiative gave Ben the drive to prove his family wrong. Mimm, his sister, did not turn loose of those investments, until Ben began to improve himself by 1925.

---

[6] Family Record- Oral family history

Transformer to increase the line voltage to 69Kv being hauled up the old Black Canyon road.

In 1925, the voltage was changed at Rock Springs switching station, which served electricity to the Kay Copper Mine. The voltage was increased from forty to sixty-nine thousand volts.

In 1926, the old obsolete one room schoolhouse, built in 1887, was closed by Yavapai County officials.

The empty building was burned by a fire of unknown origin. Ben donated Rock Springs land and materials to build a new school, where his children and grandchildren, would attend, and he would serve on the school board.

Mary Altia is born to Ben and Ruby, September 27, 1927[7]. This is the only major event occurring for the Warners in 1927. Business at Rock Springs is going well.

On July 12, 1928, Ben applies for water rights to Rock Springs (the land). As the 1920's, end Ben and Ruby had four children losing one at childbirth. Ben purchased from his in-laws the Squaw Valley Ranch[8]. The Jones family moved to the Phoenix area to build a new business there.

In the 20's, in many places there were no gas pumps; gasoline was sold in cans. Much of Ben's General store business was selling gas.

His major customer was the Kay Mine, as most of their machinery was gas-powered generators, drilling rigs, trucks and air pumps etc.

---

[7] Family History - Oral

[8] Family Record- Oral family history

In addition, the operating machinery also required different grades of oils and grease. In 1928, Ben built the gas station in front of the General Store at Rock Springs. Tom Miller[9] supplied gasoline to Ben at his general store and later at the station. The original tent store has now grown to a general store, a hotel, a pool/dance hall, and the new gas station.

Tom Miller gasoline supplier

A gold mine claim and water rights enhanced Ben's ability to keep Rock Springs independent of Cañon. Ben's 40 acres of land north of Phoenix, near the village of Glendale only added to his empire.

---

[9] Family Record- Oral family history

At the end of the 1920's Ben's hard work paid off and Rock Springs was beginning to thrive. Frank Castle, a miner and regular customer of Rock Springs is standing beside a Rock Springs fountain.

Frank Castle

Frank was typical as a customer since the major source of Ben's customers was the population of the surrounding communities including local mines, and the ranchers.

ROCK SPRINGS
ANOTHER BEGINNING

For the Warners, the 1920's, were a prosperous time. Ben, Ruby, and children started homesteading in a company tent while putting claim to the land. While homesteading the land they were also building a business, though this may seem like success to some, it took its toll on the Warner family.

Their third child died at birth. Ruby worked as hard, as a wife could. Ben worked two jobs; his own business and as an assistant superintendent for the Kay Mine after he quit Arizona Power Company.

Ad for the Arizona Power Company

As 1930 entered, The Arizona Power Company filed in the courts a lawsuit against the Kay Copper Mine Corporation, which included as defendants D.J. Richards, first engineer, Ben Warner, and Edward Roberts, superintendents, for the Kay Mine.

The tailings of the Kay Copper Mine

AUTHORS NOTE: TAILINGS (ABOVE) ARE THE WASTE OF THE ORE THAT WAS PULVERIZED TO RETAIN THE METAL OF THE ORE, WHICH WAS SOUGHT. IN THIS CASE, THE METAL THAT WAS EXTRACTED WAS COPPER AND IRON. THESE TAILINGS ARE SEEN WEST OF THE AQUA FRIA RIVER IN BLACK CANYON CITY.

This plate covers the Kay Copper Mine shaft entrance.

Kay Copper Mine entrance today.

With these pressures and expecting, Ruby Warner decided to leave Ben. Ben and Ruby's child, Emma Lee, was born in February 16, 1931, in Mayer after the divorce.

Richards and Warner were owed an estimated $1,675.15, in back pay. Together they filed in court against the Kay Copper Mine Corporation, on June 3, 1930. The funds owed to these two, was much less than the mine owed the power company, which was $5,623.37.

The Richards, Warner suit took the courts much less time in litigation than the power company law suit.

Yavapai County Sheriff, G.C. Ruffner, served foreclosure notice to the Kay Mine, forcing its closing. He confiscated equipment, for the court action in defense of Richards and Warner.

On July 1, 1930, Ruffner held a sheriff's auction to collect money owed Richards and Warner. The sum received from the auction was awarded to them.

Through the court process there was nothing Ben could do to save his marriage.

The division of property gave Ben the upstairs hotel, his home during the separation. Ruby got the house she was living in at Rock Springs.

She eventually moved to Mayer with the children; followed by a move to Phoenix, to help her family, the Jones, develop a business.

To save his business from battling law suits Ben sold 154.12 acres of land on March 23, 1931, to Demitri Albins, a new comer in the area. With this money in hand, Ben had a new beginning.

1932, is a new year for Ben Warner. The postal contracts are up. Ben makes a bid against Mrs. Pearl Helleher, who has been the Post Mistress since February 1, 1928.

In February of 1932, Benjamin Warner marries Henrietta.

On March 16, 1932, Benjamin Warner becomes Post Master of Cañon.

In 1933, Rock Springs has added a bus depot. The court litigation towards Kay Copper Mine Corporation, D. J. Richards, Ben Warner and Edward Roberts, continues.

On July 17, 1933, Demitri Albins pays the $5,623.37, to Arizona Power Company, owed by Kay Copper Mine Corporation, ending the mine's lawsuit.

This action continues the lawsuit, against the mine and Richards, Warner and Roberts.

Ben Warner
Dressed
for Success

On September 18th, 1933, the case is dismissed. Roberts, Richards, and Warner owe nothing and Albins takes over the mine.

On September 6, 1934, Bonnie Joyce is born to Ben and Henrietta. With four years of despair in the past, perhaps, prosperity is here for Ben and Henrietta.

The Warner's had a closeness to many of the pioneer families of the area and likewise. Many of the family names of association were, Cordes, Champies, McDonalds, Cleator, and later Jacka.

Bruce McDonald, a teenager in the late 1930's, remembers. *"My dad and I were going to Ben Warner's to help him butcher a steer. He had the animal in a pen by itself for a day or so. You can't do this if you are going to butcher a cow. You have to keep them together to socialize. When they isolate, they get strange. Anyway, as we showed up Ben was out in the pen. The animal came charging at him trampling him bad. Then! The old cow ran back at Ben running him down again, this time standing on him. Ben rolled over and we thought he was dead! He got up and shot the animal."* The year was about 1937.

Late in 1937, Ben petitions the United States Post Office seeking the name change of postal Cañon to Rock Springs. Ben gets his wish. February 1, 1938, the area is officially, Rock Springs.

The following is from the writings of Elizabeth Wright, who interviewed George Carlin, a former foreman with the Kay Mine[10]. *"The Kay Copper Mine, west of Cañon, opened around 1918, and employed many families. They lived in part wood and tent homes at the mine. Their children attended the Cañon School. They had two teachers Mrs. Fisher and Miss Fitzgerald, during this population of growth. Then layoffs at the mine in the late 1920's, affected school attendance. One of the teachers, Miss Fitzgerald, was dropped. Mrs. Fisher then taught all the classes in the school."*

Warner children circa
1935 (back to front)
Ben Jr., Bob, Emma
and Mary.

---

[10] Interview mid 1970's

ROCK SPRINGS GOES TO WAR

As a businessman the early years were hard on Ben. He often stuttered, and business opponents would often challenge his disability. Ben it is said, would never back down. Sometimes it would lead to fights. He came to Black Canyon, a.k.a. Cañon, with money and saw the future opportunity. As a businessman, he was strict yet open minded, with his customers. If he liked you, you got credit.

The early years his general store served miners and ranchers. Miners often paid in gold. As the sheep herders drove their sheep through Rock Springs they needed goods and had no money. Ben would accept wool and an occasional lamb for payment. Ben conformed to the times and supplied the customers with their needs[11].

In 1940, Jerry Jacka Sr., of the Sun-Up Ranch in New River, had a route delivering soda pop, from Phoenix to Prescott. Rock Springs became a big customer.

---

[11] Family oral history

Says, Jerry Jr. *"When my father, had his soda pop route Ben Warner, became one of his best customers. Ben probably had enough money, to get it anywhere. But, he liked my father and they became friends."*

Cowboys from Wranglers Roost

One fine spring Saturday in 1940, these riders visited Rock Springs. They rode from Wranglers Roost, New River. The rider far left is Pete Halle, who supplied the photo.

Many locals came from as far as Wranglers Roost, New River to trade at Rock Springs. The Halle family owned Wranglers Roost from 1941 into the 50's.

Ben Jr. was a Golden Gloves boxer before the war. His father put him into Golden Gloves because of his affinity to fight. Ben Sr. hoped this would cage his disruptive behavior by channeling his aggression to the sport. He boxed in Phoenix and was an excellent boxer.

When the U.S. entered the war in 1941, so did Robert and Ben Jr.

Robert followed his father's example and enlisted into the Navy from 1942 to 1947. When the Korean War broke out he re-enlisted.

Ben and Robert   Robert during Korean Tour

Ben Jr., enlisted into the Marines. Ben Jr. spent a hard five years in the war and beyond. It caused enough to create emotional damage through his life.

When Ben Jr. mustered out of the Marines, he came back to Rock Springs to live with the family. He was a little twisted and would get into fights, when he disagreed with people. His aggression was enough to make his father nervous and afraid to disagree with him at times.

Ben Jr., Bonnie and Ben Sr.

In the mid-1940's, Mary Reinichen who was 16, began working at Rock Springs. Her family lived at Perry Buchanan's ranch, about five miles away. Because, of the distance to work from the ranch, Ben gave her a place to stay upstairs, during the work week.

She met Bob, when he was on leave and they eventually started dating when the war was over. On October 15, 1948, they married.

According to the Bureau of Land Management, along with being a road of transportation (vehicles) and cattle drive trail beginning in 1886, was also officially designated, as a Sheep Driveway.

During the sheep drives of Black Canyon, they would either stop at Martin's General Store, which served as a sheep shearing station, or continue through to Rock Springs, on their way to New River, at the Sun-Up Ranch.

According to Bonnie, "the sheep herders would stop at Rock Springs for feed and water, on their way south to New River.

"One year, one of the herders gave me a lamb which I raised as a pet. I had it for almost a year."

Much to her disappointment, her father butchered her lamb.[12]

---

[12] Ben considered the lamb as being payment from a Sheepherder for services rendered.

Lamb & Bonnie

May 27th 1941 Ben acquired the T-J (T bar J) brand from the Jones family. This was the brand they used at the Squaw Valley Ranch in Cañon.

APPLICATION TO RE-RECORD BRANDS

Ben Warner
Cañon, Arizona

Fee $2.00

State Brand Certificate No.

Received and filed for record at Phoenix, Arizona, at _____ M.,

Entered in the State Brand Records in File _____ , this _____ day of _____ , 19____

(Above to be filled in by Board)

LIVE STOCK SANITARY BOARD,
Phoenix, Arizona

_____ , Arizona, _____ , 19____

For the purpose of complying with Sections 2113, 2114 and 2115 of Article 4 of Chapter 48, Revised Statutes of Arizona, 1928, as amended by Session Laws of 1931, I hereby make application to re-record the following brands, as the same now appear of record in your office under No. A____8353____ in State Brand Book No. 4 _____ on Page 1671 _____ , and I herewith transmit the sum of $2.00 recording fee therefor, certified copy of such record to be furnished me:

RIGHT SIDE   LEFT SIDE   RIGHT SIDE   LEFT SIDE

T-J   T-J

Location of Brand: Left Ribs   Location of Brand: Left Thigh

Location of Range: Vicinity of Black Canon, Maricopa & Yavapai Counties
State in what County, and whether in northern, eastern, southern, western or central part. On what river, creek or spring. In what valley or mountain range.

BOOKKEEPER   Name of Owner Ben Warner

MONIES RECEIVED   Street or P. O. Box No.

MAY 27 1941   City or Town Rock Springs

CHECKS   Name of Person signing for Owner

CASH 2.00   Address

Subscribed and sworn to before me, this 27th day of May , 1941

G. P. Wood

Transfer of brand record # 8353 from Jones to Ben Warner

63

September 22, 1942, Ben and Henrietta are blessed with their second child, Donna. Little else happened that year.

Margret, Donna and Bonnie

When Ben was on the school board the State, or County Government wanted to close the school because of lack of students compared to other schools.

Ben fired the current teacher and hired a new teacher, who had three children creating enough students to keep the school open.

Bonnie Warner's Class L to R: Mrs. Levitt, Barbara Levitt, David Ford, Fawn (last name unknown), Bonnie Warner, Gale Dingman, Joann Levitt, Zane Mannifee, Fern Levitt, Bob Mannifee.

Donna & Bonnie about 1946

Through the 1940's, Rock Springs served as a bus depot for the Santa Fe and Greyhound Bus Lines.

ARIZONA BUS COMPANY

AUTO TRANSIT LINES OVER THE SUPERB SCENIC
HIGHWAY BETWEEN PRESCOTT AND
JEROME—CLARKDALE, COTTONWOOD
AND CLEMENCEAU

PASSENGER, FREIGHT AND EXPRESS SERVICE

Three Passenger Stages and Two Freight Trucks Daily

Stages leave Prescott at 9:00 a.m., and at 1:00 and 5:00 p.m.
Stages leave Jerome at 9:00 a.m., and at 1:00 and 4:30 p.m.

ONE HOUR AND A HALF RUNNING TIME

Freight Trucks Leave Prescott at 12 o'clock noon, and at 4 o'clock
in the morning

Agents for Atlantic-Pacific, Black Canyon and Pickwick
Stages. Tickets on sale for points on these lines anywhere in the United States.

Arizona Bus Company

BLACK CANYON STAGE LINE
-- SCHEDULES --

White Spar	Black Canyon
SOUTH BOUND	**SOUTH BOUND**
Lv. Jerome ....3:00 p.m.	Lv. Jerome ....9:00 a.m.
Lv. Prescott ....4:30 p.m.	Lv. Prescott ....10:30 a.m.
Lv. Congress Jct. ......6:40 p.m.	Lv. Mayer ....11:45 a.m.
Lv. Wickenburg ......7:00 p.m.	Lv. Canyon ....2:00 p.m.
Ar. Phoenix ....8:45 p.m.	Ar. Phoenix ....3:45 p.m.
NORTH BOUND	**NORTH BOUND**
Lv. Phoenix ....3:15 p.m.	Lv. Mayer ....1:35 p.m.
Lv. Wickenburg ......5:00 p.m.	Lv. Phoenix ....9:15 a.m.
Lv. Congress Jct. ......5:35 p.m.	Ar. Prescott ....2:45 p.m.
Lv. Prescott ....7:40 p.m.	Ar. Jerome ....4:00 p.m.
Ar. Jerome ....9:05 p.m.	

Black Canyon Stage Line

The bus depot, at Rock Springs did not have a café so Bonnie and her mother would often make to go meals upon request.

Bonnie would help her parents by selling bus tickets and working at the post office.

In this 1946 photo the Santa Fe and Greyhound Bus Lines, logo signs hang beneath the Chevron gas company sign blowing in the wind.

Rock Springs Bus Stop

The doors beneath the air conditioning unit were, at that time, a pool/dance hall.

Today they are the doors to the main restaurant.

This is the building where the first bar was established in 1961. The building to the left was the general store post office, and bus depot. Today, it is the gift shop. Upstairs was the hotel. Today it is used as an office.

The Rock Springs Cafe entrance 2012

SR-69 was repositioned several times to the East, from 1940 until I-17 was built. Today it is officially the southbound lanes of I-17.

SR -69 in 1931

Says Bonnie, of the following panorama photo:

"This big barn, Dad used to store his heavy machinery. It was also used for doing repairs."
"About 1947, Dad sold this land to the State for road development. Along with it went the buildings and barn. They used to store road machinery in it, and I suppose the cars are from the workmen, that worked on the road."

Through these photos, we see what the Rock Springs Empire once was. The power station is in the far background.

Once it (the power station) had a house built to the north of it. The house burned down and the Black Canyon City Fire Department refused to put the fire out when they showed up.

The barn in the foreground was eventually torn down for the development of the road. Within the context of the photos, you can also see a variety of trailers, most likely for living quarters of the workmen.

Rock Springs area of the Black Canyon Hwy
1948 is clearly visible in this photo.

Panorama courtesy of Arizona State Archives

According to Bonnie, there were two men, Perry Buchanan a rancher and Frank Castle a miner, who came in daily for their mail. They would often argue about issues of the day. No one knew this but they were actually friends who loved to argue with each other.

Bonnie Warner & Frank Castle

Says Bonnie; *"Although my father had his stuttering under control, when these two would get into their arguments, and father got into it, his stutter would really come out."*

Bonnie, Perry Buchanan, Maxine Martin

Mary Reinichen (Warner) sits by the spring created pond.

Mary Warner at the igloo.

Linda Halliburton (Warner) reflects on memories of her mother Mary Reinichen (Warner) sitting in the same location as her mother decades before.

Linda Halliburton (Warner) reflects
Photo by Bob Roloff "The Arizona Duuude"

Warner's home in Squaw Valley (Black Canyon) formerly owned by the Jones family. Henrietta's parents built the home in 1916. It is still occupied today.

Henrietta, Bonnie, Mary, Ben (hidden behind Mary Warner), Mary, Donna & dog.

Bonnie is standing at the porch of her Rock Springs home.

As the 1940's end, happiness begins. Ben has his first grandchild and the beginning of the 3rd generation.

Robert and Mary are the proud Rock Springs parents of Dewayne born in 1949.

Mary holding Dewayne Warner

Dewayne, Ben & Robert – 3 generations of Warners

Donna and Bonnie entering Rock Springs

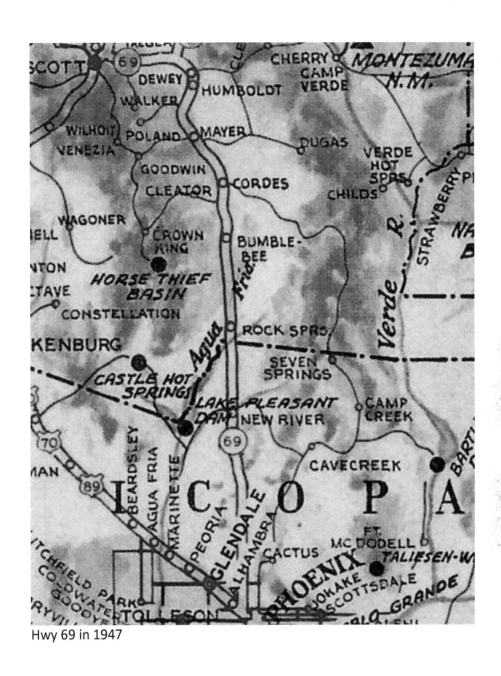

Hwy 69 in 1947

SR 69 moves farther east.

ROCK SPRINGS MOVES INTO MODERN TIMES
AS THE LEGACY ENDS

The 1950's enter with change for Ben Warner and Rock Springs. By the end of the late 1940's, the main road from Phoenix to Prescott was changing its face on the map, as well as being paved.

The old Black Canyon Road[13], which once hugged its way along the river's banks into what is todays Rock Springs parking lot. Black Canyon Road is moved further to the east, of the front door of today's restaurant, where the gas pumps were for that time.

1960 Black Canyon Hwy is paved

---

[13] Black Canyon Highway, SR 69, and Black Canyon Road, are one and the same.

In the picture below are members of the Warner family posing in front of the gas station sign. Family members are Bonnie, Uncle Jack Crowe, Aunt Mimm, (Ben's sister), and Ben.

Warner family at road sign ad along SR-69

Henrietta leaves with young Donna and Bonnie. Bonnie was instructed to follow by her mother's command and Donna chose to go with her mother.

Bonnie had recently met Lee Gholson, a cowboy working for the ranches in the Table Mesa area and they began a relationship.

Eventually after a suitable courtship, they would marry in 1954.

Henrietta suddenly leaving without notice, taking the two daughters with her created a lot of hurt with Ben.

Although, Bob and his sister Mary, were there with their families, there was nothing they could do to help Ben ease the pain because the hurt ran deep into Ben's heart.

In 1953, Bob and Mary brighten the aging Ben with a granddaughter named, Linda.

In 1954, Ben sells a major portion of Rock Springs property to El Paso Gas Company for development of transporting natural gas from northern Arizona to Phoenix.

Rock Springs gas station in 50's

That same year there is an attempted robbery at Rock Springs. The robbers were apprehended at the Gold Bug Tavern in Sunnyslope. This article is the account of the attempted robbery.

Seized At Tavern

Sunnyslope Trio Jailed As Holdup Suspects

THREE SUNNYSLOPE men suspected of planning two armed robberies and failing in the one they attempted on Black Canyon Highway yesterday, were arrested later in the day by sheriff's deputies.

Jailed after a screaming woman frightened two men out of the Sun Up Tavern, 25 miles north of Phoenix, were Johnnie Myrick, 38, of 9124 N. 12th St., and two of his neighbors, Jack Winfield, 42, and his nephew, Bill Nash, 23, both of 9230 N. 11th Ave.

SHERIFF'S Sgt. Homer Ward and Deputy Tommy Bartlett dragged Myrick from the Gold Bug Tavern in Sunnyslope yesterday afternoon when they spotted the suspected holdup car outside.

Mrs. Rose Jacka later identified Myrick as one of two men who pulled a gun on her in Sun Up Tavern about 2 p.m. She said she had screamed, frightening off the suspects. Her husband, Jerry, got the license number of the fleeing car.

Ward and Bartlett arrested Winfield and Nash at their home.

WINFIELD told Sheriff's Lieutenants Lester Jones and Martin Pintz that the Sun Up robbery attempt came after the trio lost their nerve in a plot to rob Ben's Grocery in Rock Springs.

45 miles north of Phoenix.

After meeting in a bar early yesterday, Winfield told the officers, the three men decided to "get some easy money." Winfield said he had worked in a mine near Rock Springs and thought the store would have a large sum of money on hand.

When they got there, Winfield said, his nephew and Myrick entered the store with the gun, but decided against the robbery because "too many people were there."

ON THE way back to Phoenix they decided to hold up the Sun Up, he told the investigators. Winfield said he waited in the convertible car during both times.

The pistol believed to have been used was found under the seat of the car by Bartlett. The car belonged to a friend of Myrick's, Ward said.

The three were booked in the county jail for investigation of armed robbery.

Article from Arizona Republic Feb 24, 1954
(Courtesy Arizona Archives)

May 31, 1955, Ben lost his bid to keep the U.S. Postal contract. New bidder Mrs. Alma K. Amann became the postal contractor and Postmistress.

Alma and her sister owned the grocery store beside the school across the street from the Midway Saloon. Alma changed the postal name from Rock Springs to Black Canyon.

Young Linda in front yard

Young Linda is standing in their front yard. In the background is the power station that her grandfather (Ben Warner) worked on. The power station and the house are no longer there. This area is north of the current Rock Springs Café.

As the 1950's draw to a close, Ben becomes so ill that his son Bob and daughter Mary would have to take care of him. Ben's illness would not stop him from continued development of Rock Springs.

Ben was considered to be the best mechanic in the area.   Ben began an expansion to build a body and repair shop next to the gas station, however, he would not see his job completed.

Rock Springs at the time of Ben Warner's death

Left building is the one Ben was building at the time of his death.

On July 22, 1959, Ben dies in Phoenix. An era ends for Yavapai County, as well as for Rock Springs.

Bob and Son getting gas

1960's ROCK SPRINGS

When Ben Warner died in 1959, he left Rock Springs in his will to son Robert and daughter Mary.

It is unknown why son Ben Jr. and daughters Emma, Bonnie and Donna, were left out. This was a new dawning for the Warners.

There were three houses on the Rock Springs property, where the Warner families lived.

As the Black Canyon Highway 69, continued to grow through the years, so did Rock Springs.

It has its hotel, general store and gas station, serving the local residents and travelers of the time half way in proximity of Prescott and Phoenix.

Ben Warner had good business smarts and vision.

In late 1961, after Ben Warners' estate was settled Bob and Mary built the first established bar in Rock Springs.

Through the years, the Warners would often serve meals to hungry travelers, although there was no commercial kitchen. This was true home cooking.

Mary Warner, Doug (bartender), Mary Gwilt, George Gwilt, Bob Warner 1961

The Rock Springs back bar was sold to VFW Post 1796 circa 1975. Photo by Bob Roloff "The Arizona Duuude"

In 1962, the Warner family filed with the Department of Agriculture to retain Ben's Brands in the family.

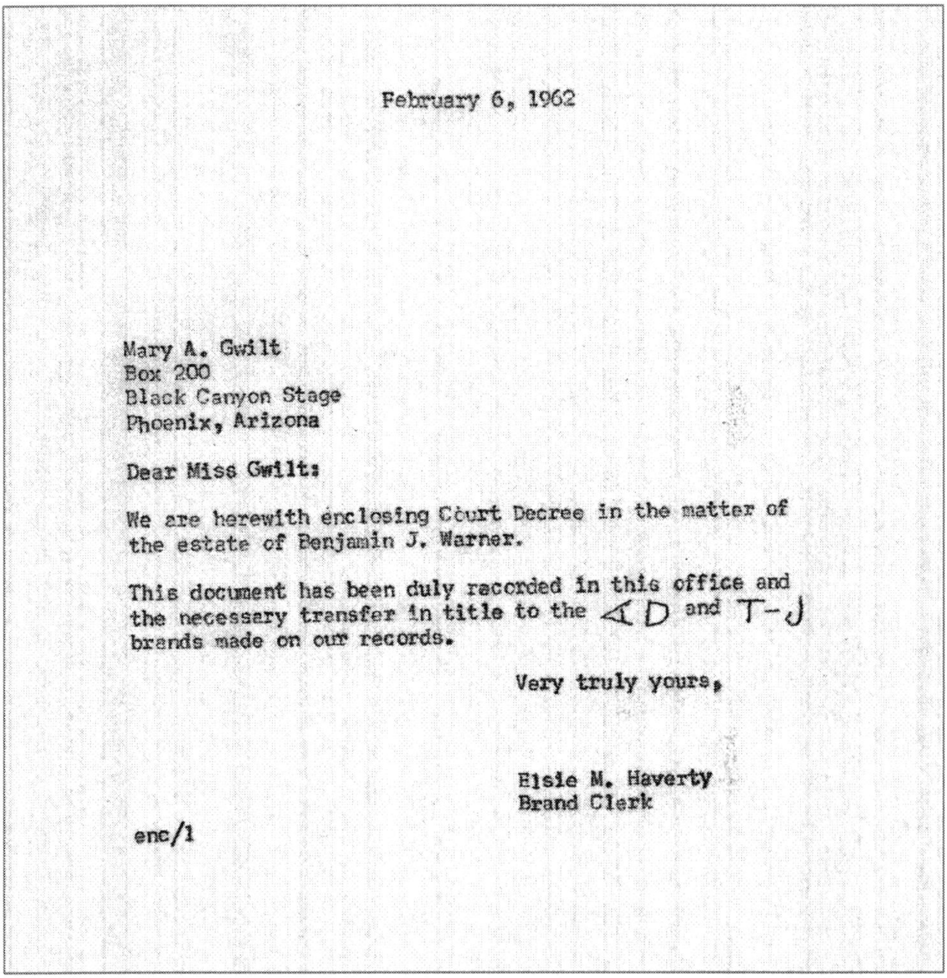

February 6, 1962

Mary A. Gwilt
Box 200
Black Canyon Stage
Phoenix, Arizona

Dear Miss Gwilt:

We are herewith enclosing Court Decree in the matter of the estate of Benjamin J. Warner.

This document has been duly recorded in this office and the necessary transfer in title to the ⊲D and T-J brands made on our records.

Very truly yours,

Elsie M. Haverty
Brand Clerk

enc/1

Letter to file Ben's Brands

In 1964, the family cafe opened as more travelers arrived, it was time to expand the cafe. The north entrance doors were removed. The bar was moved into the north room, where today's north dining room and restrooms are located.

Rock Springs store and new cafe 1964

One point of entertainment from Bob Warner is quite hilarious to a true westerner. As customers would enter the restaurant Bob would greet them with a silver serving tray with toothpicks stuck in meat. Customers enjoyed the free sample and he would point to one of the steaks on the menu, which they may order. All the while Bob enjoyed that the customers did not know they were sampling Bradshaw Mountain Oysters.

Was this the first Nut Fry for Rock Springs? The Warners raised their own cattle and butchered it for their restaurant. This further created a self-sufficiency for not depending on the neighboring Black Canyon City merchants.[14]

---

[14] Linda's story about Bob

Joe Champie's grandparents, Charles and Elizabeth Champie homesteaded in Columbia, a small mining community in southern Yavapai, in 1886.

Emma Warner and husband Joe Champie

Unlike the rest of his family who became ranchers, Joe married Emma Warner, and where he became a carpenter, settling down in Phoenix.

This is where the famous Rock Springs pies come in. Bob's sister Mary created a variety of pies for desserts. Linda would assist Mary on her making of the pies. The famous Rock Springs pies were first known as Mary's Pies. Mary was often called the pie lady. The best-selling pie was Mary's boysenberry[15].

As traffic of the freeway thickened in the 1960's and population grew in Black Canyon City, so did the business at Rock Springs. Bob had a tough decision to make about the lack of parking at Rock Springs.

He closed down the hotel, and the family moved into another location on the property, as he tore down the house and yard to make way for a larger parking lot.

In 1967, the Funk family acquired land northwest of Black Canyon City, to build a Dog Racing Track. Once again, business is good because of the influx of people attending the races.

---

[15] Arizona's official Centennial Pie

The only other eating places at the time in the vicinity of Rock Springs were the Dairy Bar, Canary Castle, and Midway Saloon. The Dairy Bar and Canary Castle were nothing more than hamburger stands.

The Midway became Ellie's Saloon, in 2005 it was sold, and renamed the Javelina Crossing.

Insert is Ellie's Frontier Saloon 2002, picture is Javalina Crossing 2012

In 1968, Bob's health prompted him to think of selling Rock Springs. His sister Mary went along with the idea. They almost sold it to Phil and Jeane Albins. Phil's father bought 154.12 acres from Ben in 1931. Nothing came of the sale.

Mary has a soda break after serving Red McDonald and companion at the General Store serving counter.

Mary, Red McDonald with unknown patron.

Serving Counter today 2012. This picture shows there is   no change in the counter over the years.

Serving Counter today 2012.

In 1969, the Squaw Peak Steak House was built across from the Dog Track north of Black Canyon City.

This new lavish dining establishment did not slow down business at Rock Springs.

By 1969, Interstate 17 was completed. It ran parallel to SR-69 from Phoenix to Cordes Junction;

I-17 is a four-lane highway adding another two lanes of traffic in each direction. This is still wonderful for Rock Springs. Freeway exit 242 northbound is created giving Rock Springs top billing on the northbound exit direction sign.

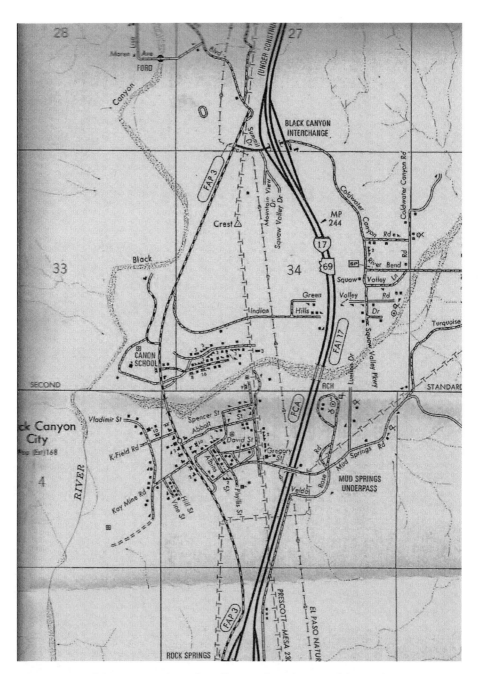

SR 69 in 1967 has moved to the East and is the southbound
 lane of I-17

WARNER FAMILY MOVES
ROCK SPRINGS FOR SALE

As 1972, dawns, Bob and his wife Mary decide to sell their share of Rock Springs, after fifty-one years of the Warner family's service to the public.

After two heart attacks and getting cancer, Bob and his wife Mary, decide it is time to take care of ones' self. The idea to pass down the family business to the grandchildren of Ben Warner was discussed. It didn't happen, as the grandchildren had other interests.

Bob's share of Rock Springs business was sold to new comers, the Harmans. Jack and Lois Harman and their son Mike from California are heirs to a jewelry store chain.

Mary Warner (Clements) decides to keep her share and she stayed at Rock Springs for another four years, making her famous pies, keeping the hospitality of the Warner family, and the Rock Springs tradition.

As travelers along I-17 discover Rock Springs, business continues to develop from the freeway traffic.

The Harman's developed business in Black Canyon City building Harmil Plaza, which had several rental spaces for businesses, including the community's first bank; The Valley National Bank.

The Valley National Bank was one of Arizona's oldest banks established in the 1920's. In the plaza was also realtors and Turpins Insurance.

The Harman's eventually became real estate developers, building the first senior care facility in Black Canyon. The health care center was never purchased and sat idle for years. It was redesigned and developed into storage facility about 1989. The storage facility was profitable and they expanded it across the street.

As the Harman's real estate prospered, so did the profits of Rock Springs, as expected.

1985, is the year the Harman's sell Rock Springs to Jack Exum and Bob Yeager. They are the leaders of an investment group of retired airline pilots.

When Bob Warner met with Jack Exum and Jack Webb taking them on a tour of Rock Springs in anticipation of selling the property he spoke passionately of the Warner family history.

Bob preferred Exum over Harman, as owner to the past family business. Harman promised all kinds of restoration that never happened.

Instead, Harman tore down stonework, like the Rock Springs fountain built by Bob's father Ben.

Rock Springs Fountain (Mark Gwilt in Stroller)

THE WARNER FAMILY REMEMBERS

The following are from a collection of interviews from Linda Halliburton (Warner), of her parents Bob and Mary Warner, Aunt Bonnie and Aunt Mary.

Bob Warner: When the discussion was brought up about the pond in back, now beside the patio.

"This was our swimming hole," Warner said as he approached a spring-fed pond about half the size of a backyard swimming pool. *"It was a great place to swim, but you always got bloodsuckers stuck to your skin."* Bob continues with, *"There were cowboys and Indians, and crusty old prospectors who scoured the nearby desert foothills in search of gold. They would stop by the Rock Springs General Store for supplies. In those days, the store mostly served miners and ranchers living in the desert foothills of the Bradshaw Mountains. It was stocked with saddles, chaps, gold panning instruments and horseshoes."*

Bob would continue with the hotel. *"There were seven hotel rooms above the general store. One room had movie star Jean Harlow spend the night."*

The guest register has been kept over the years.

Jean Harlow

Bob continues with, *"A lot of men from Phoenix would come up here with their girlfriends and stays in the hotel. There was one doctor who used to bring a different nurse up here every weekend."*

Mary Warner (Reinichen): Mary moved to Phoenix in 1937, from Waverly, Kansas with her parents in 1947. Her stepfather brought her and her mother to the Perry Buchanan ranch, an 80-acre ranch near the thumb and the Agua Fria River.

He wanted to lease for one year and to try to put down some roots as a farmer. As Mary says, *"You know the first thing I said when I got up here? I'd never live in this Godforsaken place. At first it was terrible here. I was only 17 at the time. But, people were really nice to me."*

The following is an interview by family member Jennifer Braun.[16] She interviewed Mary Warner recently. Mary's response: *"The Calvary used to come in and camp by the springs because the water was the spring. That's why it's called Rock Springs. The restaurant was started in the bar in about 1964. Old people were always stopping and thinking that this was a restaurant so that's what made me start the restaurant. And then I started making pie, and I was known as the pie baker."*

---

[16] CD created in 2010 provided by Mark Gwilt

Bonnie Gholson (Warner) is asked of the photo, on the Rock Springs dining room wall. For many years the residents and customers, are led to believe the man in the hat is Ben Warner.

The little girl is you. Who is the man? Says Bonnie, *"Why, that's old man Sully. We didn't know much of him. He used to talk to himself and walk everywhere. Man he loved to walk! He used to live in a shack down by the river. It must have been nine feet by nine feet. One day he came up missing. Dad and a few others went looking for him. They could never find him."*

Bonnie and old man Sully

ROCK SPRINGS I-17
THE REST STOP

When visiting Rock Springs, there is much to see. It has been the rest stop through the generations, long before the road out front was I-17.

Many of the artifacts have their own story; such as the still in the private dining room. There is nothing like good cold spring water to help make moonshine. In the mid-1960's The Warner still, was stored in the tack room, known as the basement. One day someone had stolen it. Dewayne found out who the villain was and had to go chase after the still all the way to Crown King, in order to return it to its rightful place in the basement.

Bonnie says, *"Dad used to make the stuff and sell it to the miners."*

Says Bruce McDonald, *"My father being friends with Ben If he knew the still was there he probably looked the other way."*[17]

---

[17] Bruce's father, Clyde McDonald, was a Yavapai County deputy Sheriff, 1919 to 1963.

During prohibition in America, most moonshiners made it for profit.

They made their own stills. Ben had a cold spring and grew corn, important ingredients for making moonshine.

After prohibition, Ben sold packaged liquor and beer. His still may have been the best-kept secret of the time, as he was never caught.

The still can be seen on its shelf in the bar at Rock Springs.

Ben Warner's Still

Through this office door was the Cañon U. S. Post Office.

Dutch door is where residents picked up their mail. Insert is the Post Office boxes.

In the 1960's when the restaurant opened, it was used as the food prep and dish washing room. Today it is the office.

Through another door was the hotel. This is where Hollywood actress Jean Harlow spent the night. The room she stayed is decorated as the "Jean Harlow Room". Her name is on the Rock Springs guest register.

Jean Harlow Room - Door on left and room interior on right.

Many Hollywood legends have visited Rock Springs such as Fred MacMurray, Jane Russell, and Tom Mix.

Jane Russell

Tom Mix

During the early 1970's when Dick Van Dyke filmed his TV show in Carefree, *He would often visit here on weekends and visited with my Dad,* says, Linda Warner.

During March 2006, Hollywood filmed the movie titled, *"Resume Speed"* staring actor, Gary Busey, at Rock Springs.

Busey discussing a scene with an actress

Gary Busey with local friends.

The Farmers Market, which sells the best produce in the area, was the Warner's first home. Ben built three homes on the property. The rental cabins built in the 1940's, today are used for businesses.

Herbs And More is an herbal shop located there. This is a great place to buy herbs, spice in bulk, and other therapeutic needs.

Building in the picture below is the original Warner home.[21]

Warner House 1989

---

[21] The Pergola roof above the Warner house is common in the southwest. It is a slated structure that protects from the relenting rays of the Arizona sun.

Authors Note: Herbs and More store has an assorted array of wonderful herbs, spices and souvenirs.

Herbs and More building 2012

Herbs and More inside store 2012

In the Rock Springs saloon built in 1987, by the Exum owners is the Brunswick Bar. The Exum family discovered the 1858 Brunswick Bar owned by a farmer, who had it stored in a barn for many years. The bar was made in Brunswick , Maine, and brought to California, by a ship going around the horn.

During Prohibition, the family that closed the saloon put it into storage, where it remained through the generations. Jack Exum found it by luck and brought it to Rock Springs.

Brunswick Bar

The back bar the Exum family bought is newer than the Brunswick Bar; it was built in the 1870's.

The outdoor patio was built in 1986, during the Exum ownership. It has been used for weddings, school proms, and special events. At present, it is used for first of the month Hog's In Heat Nut Fry.

The stone came from the Burfind Hotel, located in ghost town Gillett, at the time of building the patio.

Rock Springs Patio

The Arizona Duuude is there most weekends including the monthly Nut Fry, to take you on a walking tour.

You will go past the hotel door, see the original well, Ben Warner's home and much more.

Are you a lite eater? Ask for the Arizona Duuude breakfast in the dining room.

Arizona Duuude photo by LeeAnn Sharpe

Rock Springs employee Neal Miller had business interest with a partner owning claims at Gillett. Neal was also a gold miner.

The last known person who lived at the hotel in, 1947, was Neal who died in 1995[18]. His portrait painted by local artist Ester Britan, hangs in the saloon on the memory wall.

Neal Miller Portrait on the memory wall

[18] Arizona Highways April 1995 interviewed Neal about Rock Springs, he died in July.

Rock Springs gift shop today

Inside the main entrance is the former general store. Now it is the gift shop. To the right as you enter is the service counter, which has been in the same place since it was built in the 1920's.

Beyond the counter and to the right is the entrance to the café. At the rear is the display case for the famous Rock Springs Pie.

Author's Note: *Rock Springs is a unique rest stop because from Phoenix it is nearly half way between Flagstaff to the north and Prescott to the west. 'The Rock' as it known by locals is convenient and loved for its pie. The gift shop carries many unique Arizona items like Scorpion suckers, and nostalgic post cards.*

What is significant to the Warner family about the building in this photo?

The small door below the window is where the family tack room was. When the bar opened this is where the refrigerator was that stored beer.

One-day mid-1960's, Dewayne and a friend hoisted a few six packs of beer through the top window, and friends had a party.

They got caught.

Warner home during construction of the parking lot

This is the old Black Canyon Road coming from the north. It was also the stagecoach route.

Black Canyon Road looking north above, looking south below

Black Canyon Road looking south. The road continued past the front doors of Rock Springs, it continued southward past the cabins.

Old Black Canyon Road (SR- 69) ran a few hundred feet west of the current Interstate 17 location.

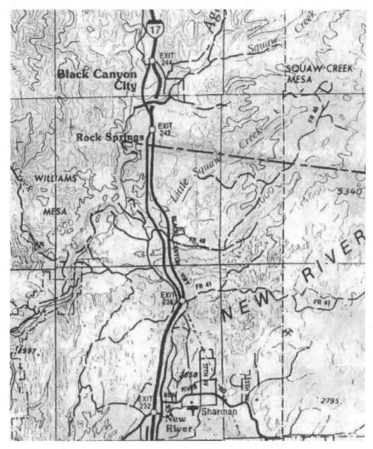

Black Canyon Road continues to move to the east

The memory wall photos, located in the main saloon, are of significance to the community of Black Canyon City. These photos of the people may seem to be only past patrons of Rock Springs, but many of them were important people in the community and Arizona. Elmer King was a past State Senator 1958-1964, as well as a business owner. John Whitson was a past employee, one of the early founders of the Black Canyon Fire Department, fire Chief, town business owner and shared the Maggie Mine with his wife Amy, who worked at Rock Springs from 1971 to 2000. Amy also grew up in Black Canyon, at The Maggie Mine. The cane (on the wall upper right) came from Troy Sharp. Past owner Jack Exum is on the wall too.

Waiting in line for the famous "Rock Springs Pie" is common around holidays.

Line to pick up pies at Rock Springs

Jerry Padgett, a valued customer of the Rock Springs Café, is from Black Canyon City. He is sitting at the Café Counter, which was the original location of the original bar.

Rock Springs Cafe Counter 2012

It is now located at the VFW in Black Canyon City. Notice the Rock Springs Pies on the chalkboard.

Ben Warner had great business foresight when he purchased the land and water rights to Rock Springs.

His legacy has lived through 2012 and will continue for a long time.

ACKNOWLEDGEMENTS

A special thank you goes to Bonnie Warner Gholson, daughter of Benjamin Warner; Linda Halliburton, granddaughter and her son Pat, great-grandson of Benjamin Warner. Dewayne Warner, Mark Gwilt, Mary Clemets, Ben Jr., Emma Warner Champie. Without the assistance of the Warner Family this book would not have been possible.

Additional thanks go to Jerry Jacka Jr. of New River and the Rim Country, Bruce McDonald of Cordes Junction, Rosalynn Fernwood of Mayer, and Pete Pelle by way of Jim Delitoso.

In addition thanks also go to Richard Shaw of the new Rock Springs, Sid Hagel editor of the first edition, Marielle Marnes, Dottie Helgeson, and LeeAnn Sharpe, editor of the second and third editions.

Special thanks are to Connie Wright for the contributions of Elizabeth Wright's writings. Inky (Publisher) and Arizona Duuude have provided valuable time supporting this project.

And most of all thanks Mom.

EPILOGUE

When Ben Warner came to Arizona, it was a new State only eight years old, new territory, with young dreams of prosperity. Ben Warner as it seems left from a State established, chasing after the dreams for a new start in life, burning a past life of despair. His Rock Springs property started out at 40 acres of land, eventually to nearly 400 acres. No one living knows what his goals were. But, for the Black Canyon area, Rock Springs was all things possible. He first sold 154.12 acres to Albins. Then another majority of the property was sold to the State for highway.

Development in 1948, caused the Rock Springs dynasty to continue to diminish. Finally by the mid 1960's, the family of Ben Warner loses all the land east of the business to the State of Arizona to the development of I-17 highway. For southern Yavapai County Arizona, Ben Warner was the first to put Rock Springs on the map. Other than his business and ranch, the post office, school district and electoral precinct were named Rock Springs.

HOWDY!!

Elaine Bonds rides the Bull at Rock Springs

Until our trails meet again.

To order additional copies of
Rock Springs Arizona History Series by
Michael Sandford with Forward by Terry
Earp and Testimonials by Marshall Trimble,
Dolan Ellis, and Bob Roloff.

Visit www.azphm.com/sandford

Also find Michael Sandford's additional
books in the Arizona history Series
including : The Last Stage Coach Ride and
Black Canyon City.

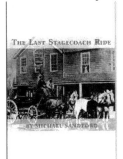

22712798R00078

Made in the USA
Columbia, SC
01 August 2018